THDRAWN

GOLF
BASICS
by Roger Schiffman

Drawings by
Robert Schoolcraft

with Photographs

Created and Produced by
Arvid Knudsen

PRENTICE-HALL, Inc.

Englewood Cliffs, New Jersey

Other **Sports Basics Books** in Series

Text copyright © 1986 by Roger Schiffman and
    Arvid Knudsen
Illustrations Copyright © 1986 by Arvid Knudsen

Printed in the United States of America   · J

Prentice-Hall International (UK) Limited, London
Prentice-Hall of Australia, Pty. Ltd., Sydney
Prentice-Hall of Canada, Inc., Toronto
Prentice-Hall·Hispanoamericana, S.A., Mexico
Prentice-Hall of India Private Ltd., New Delhi
Prentice-Hall of Japan, Inc., Tokyo
Prentice-Hall of Southeast Asia Pte. Ltd., Singapore
Whitehall Books Limited, Wellington, New Zealand
Editora Prentice-Hall do Brasil Ltda., Rio de Janeiro

10 9 8 7 6 5 4 3 2 1

Library of Congress Cataloging in Publication Data

Schiffman, Roger, 1955–
    Golf basics.

    Summary: Introduces the essential rules, equipment,
and strokes of golf and discusses how and where to play.
    1. Golf—Juvenile literature. [1. Golf]
I. Schoolcraft, Robert, ill. II. Knudsen, Arvid.
III. Title.
GV965.S275   1986   796.352'3   85-28165
ISBN 0-13-357955-7

CONTENTS

Photo Credits:
All the photographs in this book were graciously lent from the *Golf Digest* library collection.

JACK NICKLAUS AS A BOY

INTRODUCTION

Golf is a game for a lifetime—and you're never too young to learn to play.

In fact, boy or girl, the younger you are when you start playing golf and developing your golf swing, the easier the game will be when you are older. If you can attain good swing habits now—and we'll discuss how in the chapters to come—you will no doubt experience many years of enjoyment.

Some of the best golfers in the world started playing the game at an early age. Tom Watson began putting at age 6 and was playing 36 holes a day by the time he was 10. Jack Nicklaus, at age 16, already had won the Ohio Open. Nancy Lopez won the first of three straight New Mexico State Amateur championships at age 12.

But the majority of golfers rarely play in formal competition. They simply play golf for fun—with friends, family, even people they've just met at the course. And this social aspect is what playing golf is all about. But if you're interested in the competitive side, you can look forward to professional, amateur, senior, junior, men's, women's, national, state, and local tournament competition.

Golf has many fringe benefits. You can play in natural surroundings —in fresh air, among birds, trees, fields, near lakes, streams, even by the ocean.

You don't need a whole team of people to play. You can participate in a foursome, a threesome, a twosome, or even play by yourself when the course isn't crowded. You can practice alone, striving to become better and better at a sport that is impossible to master but always compels you to try.

I hope this book will instill in you the "golf bug," which bit me when I was 12 years old. It has been biting me ever since.

Roger Schiffman

JACK NICKLAUS TODAY

1 | A Short History of Golf

When compared with such sports as baseball, football, and basketball, golf is a very old game. Most sports we play today are less than 150 years old, but golf is at least 400 years old, dating back to the sixteenth century in Scotland. Records show that the first official rounds of golf were played in 1577. But it is probable that golf actually was played many years before, at St. Andrews, Scotland—most likely the oldest course in the world and considered the Home of Golf. The first national championship—the British Open—was contested in 1860, some 40 years before the first World Series.

No one knows for sure how golf originated. One theory holds that the game evolved from shepherds hitting rocks off the ground with their staffs. Perhaps the rocks from time to time went into holes made by burrowing

JOHN REID, THE "FATHER OF AMERICAN GOLF "

animals; hence, the idea for a game in which a player *tries* to knock a ball into a hole in the ground using the fewest number of strokes possible (the basic idea of golf). Another theory contends that the game came to Scotland from Holland. In Holland, a game similar to golf was once played on ice, using a stick and a ball.

However the game originated, it quickly gained popularity after that first British Open was played at Prestwick, on the west coast of Scotland. Willie Park, Sr., won that championship with a 36-hole score of 174. Such a number would not nearly be good enough today to contend in the British Open. But 125 years ago, the balls and clubs used were far inferior to what modern golfers play with.

Clubshafts 100 years ago were made of hickory wood; today they are made of steel or graphite. The balls were much lighter (often stuffed with feathers) and therefore were blown off-line by the wind. They didn't fly or roll as far and true as today's hard rubber balls do. And the courses back then were not nearly as well maintained as they are today—the greens often were rutted and uneven. Today they are usually as smooth as carpets.

FRANCIS OUIMET

In the 1890s golf came to America, brought here by such people as John Reid, considered the Father of American Golf. Reid and his Apple Tree Gang built the first course in America—three holes in an apple orchard at Yonkers, New York—and called it St. Andrews, after St. Andrews in Scotland. Some friends from other courses on the East Coast and Chicago formed the United States Golf Association (USGA) in 1894, and the first U.S. Open and U.S. Amateur championships were played the next year in Newport, Rhode Island.

The American game grew in popularity among the elite when such professional players as Harry Vardon and Ted Ray came over from Britain to play in American tournaments and exhibitions. But when Francis Ouimet, an American amateur, beat Britain's finest golfers to win the U.S. Open in 1913, the sport gained national prominence. Its popularity has been growing ever since.

ARNOLD PALMER

BOBBY JONES

Of course, other great tournament players contributed to the game's enormous rise in popularity. Walter Hagen, Sam Snead, Gary Player, Patty Berg, Babe Didrickson Zaharias, and Mickey Wright each played a role. Also contributing to this phenomenal growth were several organizations other than the USGA: The Professional Golfers' Association (PGA) and the PGA Tour (a separate body of tournament professionals), the LPGA Tour (women professionals), and the National Golf Foundation (NGF). Just in the past 35 years the number of golfers in this country has increased from 3.2 million to about 18 million, and the number of courses from 5,000 to 13,000.

Golf is fortunate in that over the years its top players were not only great golfers but great people as well, showing that golf is a universal bridge for good sportsmanship and camaraderie. Every decade has had its stars: Bobby Jones in the 1920s, Gene Sarazen in the '30s, Byron Nelson in the '40s, Ben Hogan in the '50s, Arnold Palmer in the '60s, Jack Nicklaus in the '70s, and Tom Watson in the '80s. Palmer, especially, with his charging, go-for-broke-no-matter-what style, is similarly credited with capturing the imagination of the average American and bringing golf, with the help of television, into the limelight. Nancy Lopez is similarly credited with popularizing women's golf in the last few years.

Who's next? Seve Ballesteros of Spain and Bernhard Langer of West Germany are probably the two best players in the world today, which shows that golf has become an international game, with leading players coming from Australia (Greg Norman), Japan (Isao Aoki), and even China (T.C. and T.M. Chen). Maybe the next great player will be you.

2 | How to Get Started

One of the most difficult things about playing golf as a youngster is finding a place that will allow you to play.

At least until recently, many adults didn't want children on the golf course. Fortunately, that attitude is changing in many parts of the country as a number of club pros and recreation departments are emphasizing golf for juniors, to make sure that golf as a game for everyone will continue to grow and prosper.

The best place for young people to play golf is at a municipal course or country club in their area. If your family belongs to a country club, you probably can play there. People who are not members of such clubs can play at public courses.

If you aren't sure if there is a municipal course in your area, check the Yellow Pages of the phone book. Such courses should be listed with addresses and phone numbers. Call before going to the course to be sure there are no restrictions on juniors playing. Often, municipal courses will allow juniors to play at reduced rates during certain hours. Ask about that when you call.

Also listed in the phone book are driving ranges where you can hit buckets of balls, even at night under lights, without ever going to a real course.

Perhaps some of your relatives play golf. Ask if you may join them some time. You might want to walk around with them and not play at first, just to get a better understanding of the game.

AMY ALCOTT (FAR LEFT) AT AGE 10.

One of the best ways to get started in golf is by being a caddie. Many country clubs and other courses hire youngsters eager to make some extra money. Call the courses in your area and ask to speak to the head pro or the caddie master. He can tell you if they have a caddie program or, if not, which courses do.

A summer spent caddying is rewarding in several respects: (1) You can make money (often as much as $10 to $20 per round, depending on the area of the country you live in); (2) You may be allowed to play the course for free on Mondays or on other days when the course is closed or uncrowded; (3) You can meet some very influential adults who might help you later when you're looking for a permanent job.

Many top players in history started as caddies. Ben Hogan and Seve Ballesteros credit their early caddie days with teaching them the basics of the game and influencing them toward careers in golf.

If you want to hit golf balls and there are no courses or driving ranges in your immediate area, you might try going to a deserted football field or an open pasture to practice hitting shorter shots. But if you do this, always be sure that other people aren't around who might get hit with a stray shot. Also, don't hit balls near windows or cars. Broken glass is not only dangerous, it's very expensive to replace.

How to Get Clubs

Once you've found a place to play, you need to get some clubs and balls to play with. Again, ask the pro at the course in your area. Perhaps he has an old set of clubs that he no longer needs. He may be happy to cut them down to your size and give them to you or sell them at a low price.

If you have a bit more money to spend (perhaps from caddying), you can buy a set of junior clubs at a sporting goods store or golf shop. If possible, try to get a professional to fit you with the correct length. Ask him or her if the grip thickness is correct for your size hands and if the overall weight of the clubs is about right, too.

The PGA (Professional Golfers' Association) of America runs a program called Clubs for Kids. Perhaps the professional in your area participates and can give you some clubs from this national organization.

You don't need a full set of clubs to start with. A 5-iron and putter is all you need. As you progress and play more, you can add clubs to your bag: a 7-iron next, then a 9-iron, then a 5-wood and a 3-wood, until eventually you have a full set. Or you can buy the odd-numbered clubs and a bag at a golf shop or sporting goods store. Such a set costs from $50 to $100.

You also can buy golf balls at a sporting goods store or golf shop or you can find them in the rough and woods of a course at the end of the day when no one is playing. You may be surprised at how many golf balls are lost in the rough.

WALTER KELLER TEACHING HIGH SCHOOL KIDS.

14

How to Get Instruction

Once you have some clubs and balls and a place to hit them, you probably will want to find someone who can give you some lessons, someone who knows a lot about the golf swing.

Many recreation departments have golf classes for juniors, as do local Y's. Or ask the golf pro at a course or driving range nearby.

If a parent or other relative plays golf, perhaps he or she can give you some basic instruction. But, in general, it's better to learn from someone you don't know as well. It's easier to learn from someone you're not trying to please or impress. Such a teacher is freer to give you constructive criticism.

The number of lessons to start with depends on how much time and money you want to spend. Generally, a set of three to five lessons is about right to start with. Then a follow-up lesson every month or so will keep you progressing along the right track.

You also can read golf books and magazines to learn golf terminology and to get ideas about the correct way to swing. These publications also are excellent for helping you learn about golf strategy on the course.

Lessons from a golf professional can be expensive—about $20 a half hour. At Y's and recreation departments they are considerably cheaper. If you really want lessons from a golf professional but can't afford them, one possibility is to ask him or her if you can help out around the golf shop, taking care of golf carts and cleaning members' clubs in exchange for free lessons.

You also might consider attending a junior golf camp. There are more than 30 week-long camps around the country. These usually are listed in the spring issues of the national golf magazines. They range in price from $250 to $750, including instruction, playing time, and room and board.

Wherever and however you find instruction, remember: Good teaching alone will not make a better golfer. It also takes practice and lots of dedicated hard work. Golf is not an easy game. But the harder you work at it, the more fun—and rewarding—it will be.

AMY ALCOTT TODAY IN COMPETITION

3 | The Language of Golf

Golf, like any other sport, has its own vocabulary. Here is a list of common words and phrases used in golf that you should be familiar with when you start playing. Don't feel you have to memorize them now. You will learn what each one means as you spend more and more time around other golfers.

Address—Putting the body and club in position to hit the ball. Also called setup.

Ball position—Where the ball is located in relation to your feet in the setup.

Clubface—The part of the club that meets the ball in hitting a shot. The face usually has grooves.

Clubhead—The heavier part of the club opposite the grip end. It usually is made of wood on a "wood" club and metal on an "iron" club. Some modern "wood" heads are actually made of metal and are called "metal woods."

Divot—A piece of turf that is cut from the ground by the club during a shot.

Dogleg—A hole with a fairway that curves to the right or to the left.

Driver—The No. 1 wood. This club is used for maximum distance. Usually it is used with the ball teed on a tee peg so the ball is off the ground.

Fairway—The part of a golf hole between the tee and the green where the grass is cut short. This area is where the ball should land from the teeing ground, as opposed to in the rough.

Golf course—The entire area used to play golf, including tees, greens, fairways, hazards, rough, and trees.

Green—Putting surface where the grass is cut the shortest and where the cup and flagstick are placed.

Handicap—A numerical rating of a golfer in relation to par. The lower your handicap, the better a player you are. Handicap is also the term used for rating holes according to difficulty. The lower the handicap figure, the more difficult the hole.

Hazard—Any bunker or water (lakes, rivers, streams, ocean) on the golf course.

Hook—A shot that curves from right to left (for a right-handed golfer).

Iron—Any club, except the putter or metal wood, with an iron or steel head.

Loft—The amount of slant in the face of a club. The greater the loft, the higher and shorter the shot.

Out of bounds—Outside the playing area of the course, usually marked by white stakes.

Pull—A shot that starts to the left of the target (for a right-handed golfer).

Push—A shot that starts to the right of the target (for a right-handed golfer).

Putter—A club with minimal loft used to roll the ball on the green.

Rough—The area of the course where the grass is long, usually bordering the fairway.

Sand trap—A hazard on the course that is usually a large hole with sand in the bottom. Also called a sand bunker or bunker.

Sand wedge—An iron with more loft than a pitching wedge, with a large flange for hitting out of sand bunkers and for hitting very high and short shots from turf.

Scorecard—A card used to write down your score. It also provides information about the course, such as the par and yardages of each hole, the handicap of each hole, and sometimes a diagram of the course.

Setup—See Address.

Slice—A shot that curves to the right (for a right-handed golfer).

Stance—How the feet are placed in relation to the target line and to the ball.

Target line—An imaginary line extending from the ball to the target.

Tee—A peg, usually made of wood or plastic, on which the ball rests for a shot from the teeing area. Also, the grassy area where the first shot is made on each hole.

Wedge—An iron with greater loft than a 9-iron that is used for short, high shots.

Wood—A club whose head is made of wood. Some modern "woods" are actually made of metal, graphite, ceramic, or other material.

4 | How Golf Is Played

The object of the game of golf is to hit a ball with a club from Point A (the teeing ground) to Point B (the fairway) to Point C (the green) into Point D (the hole) in the fewest number of strokes possible.

A normal round consists of 18 *holes* (the teeing ground, fairway and rough, hazards, and green comprise a hole). The player with the fewest number of strokes to complete the 18 holes wins. That person is said to have the lowest score.

Golf is different from other sports in that a lower score is better than a higher score. For instance, if you make a 5 on a hole and your friend makes a 6, you made the better score.

There are basically three types of holes on a golf course: par 3's, par 4's, and par 5's. The par 3's are the shortest holes. It is possible (for better players probable) to hit your ball onto the green in one stroke. Then if you can knock your ball into the cup in two more strokes (*putts*), your total score for the hole is a 3. A 3 on a par-3 hole is called a *par*.

On a par-4 hole, it is possible to reach the green in two shots. If you do this and take two putts to knock the ball into the cup, you have a 4, or a par.

On a par-5 hole, the longest of the three types of holes, it is possible to hit the green in three shots. Then if you take two putts, you have made a 5, or a par.

If you score one stroke less on a hole than its par, you have made a *birdie* (a 2 on a par 3, for instance, or a 4 on a par 5). A birdie is one under par. If you score one stroke more on a hole than its par, you have made a *bogey* (a 5 on a par 4, for instance). A bogey is one over par. Two under par is called an *eagle* (a 3 on a par 5, for example), and two over par is a *double bogey* (a 5 on a par 3). Three over par is a *triple bogey*, four over par a *quadruple bogey*, and so on.

A GOLF HOLE

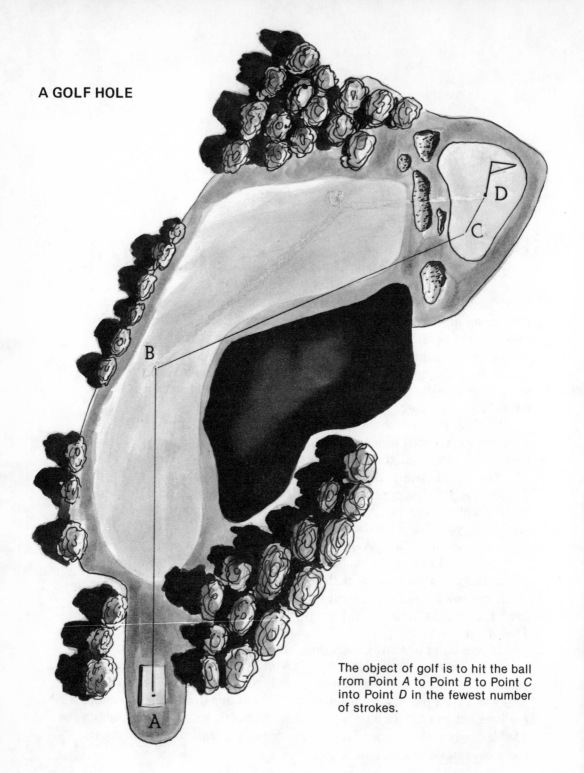

The object of golf is to hit the ball from Point *A* to Point *B* to Point *C* into Point *D* in the fewest number of strokes.

The par of a hole is usually determined by the hole's length. General-ly, a par 3 is up to 249 yards. A par 4 is 250 to 469 yards; a par 5 is more than 469 yards.

While some people consider a round to be 18 holes, you can play just nine holes at a time and keep nine-hole scores. Most courses have 18 holes, but sometimes courses consist of only nine holes. When golfers play nine-hole courses, they often play them twice to make an 18-hole round.

In one form of golf, called *stroke play*, you keep track of your total score for nine holes or for 18. Another form of scoring is called *match play*. In this format, you play your opponent, and see who gets the lowest score, hole by hole, and do *not* keep track of your total score. In match play, you are concerned only with winning or tying one hole at a time. The player who wins the most holes in the round wins the match. For instance, if you make a 5 on the first hole and your opponent makes a 7, you win the hole and are said to be 1-up. When you are up more holes than you have left to play (4-up with three holes remaining, for example), you have won the match.

Basic Rules

The rules of golf are quite complicated and are covered in detail in a book published by the United States Golf Association. If you know a few basic rules, however, you can handle almost any situation that might occur when you're playing. (It's always a good idea to keep a small rules book in your golf bag. These books can be bought from a local golf professional or can be ordered from the USGA.)

The most important rule is that you are not allowed to touch your ball once it is in play until it is on the green. When your ball is on the putting surface, you may mark it with a coin or a ball marker and pick it up. When you mark your ball on the green, place the coin or ball marker directly behind the ball. When you replace your ball, put it back exactly where it was and pick up the coin or ball marker.

If you lose your ball after it is in play on a hole or hit it out of bounds, you must take a *stroke-and-distance penalty*. You must count the original stroke plus a penalty stroke and then replay the shot, counting that stroke as well. For instance, if you hit your tee shot out of bounds, you must replay the shot and are hitting 3 (your original shot plus a penalty shot and your next tee shot).

If you hit your ball into a water hazard, it is a one-stroke penalty unless you try to hit the ball out of the water, in which case there is no penalty stroke. You have three options when you hit into the water: (1) You can

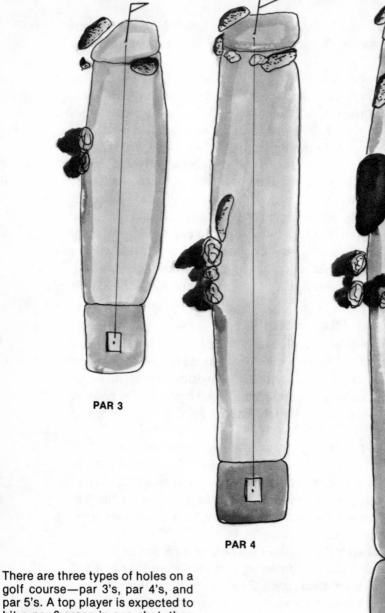

PAR 3

PAR 4

PAR 5

There are three types of holes on a golf course—par 3's, par 4's, and par 5's. A top player is expected to hit a par-3 green in one shot, then take two putts for a regulation par (left). A top player should hit a par 4 in two shots (center) and a par 5 in three shots (right), each time taking two putts for *regulation pars*.

play the shot from the water (usually very risky); (2) You can rehit the shot from the place where you hit the ball into the water, counting a one-stroke penalty when you drop another ball; and (3) You may drop a ball on an imaginary line from the hole through the point where the ball went into the water, going as far back along that line as you want. If it is a *lateral* water hazard, you may drop another ball within two club lengths from the point where the ball crossed the margin of the hazard, no closer to the hole.

When you are in a hazard (water, sand bunker, some grass bunkers) you are not allowed to let your club touch the ground or water until you start your downswing. If you do, it is a two-stroke penalty.

Golf is a unique game in that its rules are based on the honor system. That is, golfers must police themselves, because in friendly competition there are no referees, umpires, or officials. Sometimes you must call a penalty on yourself because you may be the only person on the course who knows you broke a rule.

For instance, if you are in a sand bunker and accidentally *ground your club* (let it touch the sand), you should tell the others in your group and count a two-stroke penalty. That may seem a bit harsh, but you would want your opponent to do the same if he or she broke a rule. Also, if you are playing in a tournament in which there are other players competing in other groups on the course, it is your responsibility to call a rules violation on someone in your group if you see that person breaking a rule. In effect, you are looking out for all the other players in the tournament who would not be able to see the violation. If you do not call a penalty when you see a rules infraction, then you also are considered to be in violation of the rules.

So it is a good idea to be as familiar as possible with all the rules. And if you are uncertain about a possible rules violation, play a provisional ball, keep score with both balls for that hole, and ask the local pro for the correct ruling when you finish your round.

5 | Putting

Putting is perhaps the most important part of the game because it is closely related to scoring. If you are a good putter, you usually will be able to make up for a bad full-swing shot you might have made earlier on that hole. Usually the only time you putt is when your ball is on the *green* (also called the putting surface). Sometimes, if the grass is short enough and the ground smooth enough, you can putt from just off the green.

The putting stroke is relatively short—much shorter than a full golf swing. When you putt, you want the ball to roll on the green as smoothly as possible. You try to hit the ball very close to the hole, if not *in* the hole. You need a short stroke because you want to be very accurate in the direction and distance you roll the ball. Being a good putter takes lots of practice, confidence in your ability, and a good putting stroke. Here's how to develop a solid stroke:

1. Make sure you have a well-balanced putter that is the correct length for you. Ask a local golf professional or a good amateur golfer to check your putter. Its sole should lie flat on the ground as you set up to putt, with neither the toe nor the heel in the air. (See illustration.)
2. Find the "sweet spot" of your putter blade and always try to hit the ball on that sweet spot. To find the sweet spot on your putter, hold the shaft lightly at the grip end between your thumb and index finger. Then tap the blade of the putter with a pencil eraser tip, moving the eraser from the toe of the putter to the heel as you tap. When the putter doesn't vibrate but moves straight back, you are hitting the sweet spot. It is a good idea to mark that sweet spot on top of the putterhead with a file or a small piece of tape so you can remember exactly where it is. Many times the sweet spot is not in the center of the blade but closer to where the shaft joins the blade.

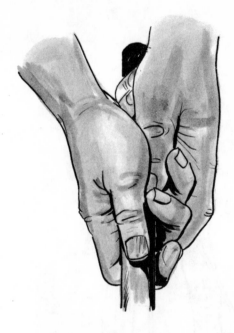

Grip the putter with your palms facing each other and the shaft resting against the lifeline of your left hand.

Make sure your putterhead lies flat on the ground, with neither the heel nor the toe in the air. The putter has minimal loft so the ball rolls smoothly on the green. Sometimes you can putt from just off the putting surface if the grass is short and the ground is smooth.

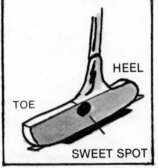

3. Grip the putter as shown in the illustration, making sure the palms of your hands are facing each other. It is best if the putter handle rests against the middle of your left palm and extends up the center of your wrist. This is called the *lifeline grip* because the putter shaft touches the lifeline of your left hand. The lifeline grip, with your palms facing each other, is preferable because it promotes a stiff-wristed stroke, rather than a loose-wristed one, and is generally easier to control.

In putting, stand to the ball so it is opposite your left heel or in the middle of your stance and your eyes are looking directly over the ball. Hold the putter with a light grip pressure and with the shaft vertical to the ground.

4. Stand so the ball is opposite your left heel or the middle of your stance and your eyes are looking directly over the ball. You can check where your eyes are located by dropping another ball from the bridge of your nose to the ground. The ball you drop should land on top of the ball you are setting up to, or are about to hit. If it doesn't, adjust your head position until the ball you drop from between your eyes lands on top of the ball on the ground. (See illustration.)

5. Practice stroking short putts first on the practice green (say five feet or less) and gradually move away from the cup until you are hitting putts up to 30 or 40 feet. The farther from the cup you get, the more important it is to concentrate on how far you need to roll the ball and the less important it is to think about the direction.

Generally, the longer the putt, the farther you should take the putter away from the ball on the backswing. Always try to follow through at least as far as the distance you take the putter back after contact with the ball. That way, your putter blade will be accelerating when it meets the ball, providing more solid contact and truer roll. When you are stroking a putt, always try to make a smooth pendulum-type swing, keeping your grip pressure light and constant throughout. Keep these thoughts in mind as you practice and see yourself performing them perfectly.

Make sure your eyes are positioned directly over the ball. To check this, drop another ball from between your eyes. It should land on top of the ball that is on the ground. If the ball you drop misses the ball on the ground, adjust your head position and drop the ball again until it hits the ball on the ground, showing that your eyes are directly over the ball.

6 | Chipping

Chipping is similar to putting in that you use a relatively short stroke and you try to hit the ball only short distances. Chipping differs from putting, however, in that you use a lofted club—6-iron, 7-iron, 8-iron, 9-iron, pitching wedge, or sand wedge—to enable you to send the ball into the air for a short period of time before it rolls to the hole.

You use this stroke when the ball is a few feet off the putting surface. The ball should roll farther than it flies in the air.

The basic chipping stroke is similar to the putting stroke. Set up to the ball as if you were putting. But your feet should be closer to the hole than they are when putting. The ball should lie opposite the area between the middle of your stance and your right foot. This places more of your weight on your left foot and positions your hands slightly ahead (toward the hole) of the ball.

The chipping motion is made with your arms and shoulders. Keep your body relatively still and keep your wrists stiff, as you do in putting. A grip with your palms facing each other will help. Some players use a putting grip to chip.

On the backstroke, allow the clubhead to come up off the ground more abruptly than in the putting stroke. Then let the clubhead strike down on the back of the ball with minimal follow-through. Keep your hands ahead of the clubhead (toward the target) throughout the stroke. The ball should pop up, land softly on the green, and then roll to the hole.

In chipping, select a club that will provide minimum air time and maximum ground time. Why? Because it's easier to judge the distance of the shot when you are rolling the ball to the hole rather than landing it there. So whenever possible you should use a less-lofted club that still allows you to land the ball on the putting surface. For example, if you have a very long chip (say, all the way across the green), you might want to use 6- or 7-irons, which have minimal loft. But if you have a short chip, say only 15 feet, you may want to use a 9-iron or pitching wedge, which have more loft. If you are faced with an especially short chip, say 10 feet and from taller grass, you may even want to use a sand wedge, which has the most loft of any of your clubs. The more loft you have, the higher the ball will fly and the shorter it will roll.

Here are some points to remember when you are chipping:

Set up to the basic chip shot as you would for a putt, except that your hands and sternum should be slightly ahead of the ball. That is, your weight should be more on your left foot, your upper body closer to the target, and the ball opposite the area between the middle of your stance and your right foot.

1. First, visualize the flight and roll of the ball before you actually select the club for the shot.

2. Determine where you want the ball to land on the green so it will roll the proper distance and along the correct line to the hole.

3. Check the way the ball is lying in the grass. (If it's sitting down in the grass or is on bare ground, you may need a club with more loft. Play the ball back in your stance, more off your right foot.)

4. Select the proper club to land the ball on the spot you picked out in Steps 2 and 3.

5. When you set up to the ball, concentrate only on hitting it with the firmness necessary to land it on the spot you picked out.

Chipping well is an art that can be learned by practicing the proper technique. You can practice chipping on the putting green, chipping a few balls to one hole, then a few to another hole, and so on. Always try to use the club with the right amount of loft to land the ball just on the green so it rolls to the hole. Good chippers usually can chip the ball close enough to the hole so that they are left with only a two- or three-foot putt. Sometimes they even hole a chip (hit the ball right into the hole) from time to time. Doing so is really fun and can turn a potentially bad score on a hole into a good score very quickly.

7 | Pitching

You should hit a *pitch shot* when you are 10 to 100 yards from the hole or if you need to loft the ball high but short. Most players use a pitching wedge or a sand wedge to pitch. In a correct pitch shot, the ball flies farther than it rolls.

As in chipping, good pitchers can turn a potentially bad score on a hole into a good score by lofting the ball close enough to the hole for a one-putt. Good pitching technique comes in handy when you are behind a small tree or a bunker and need to loft the ball quickly and have it stop on the green. This often is the case when you happen to miss the green with your approach shot.

The basic pitching stance is similar to the chipping stance discussed in Chapter 6. There are two main differences, however: (1) Generally, you should stand so the ball is directly below your sternum, in the center of your stance; (2) You should use a conventional golf grip (see illustration), the same grip you will use for all your full-swing shots, from the sand wedge to the driver.

The pitching motion is bigger than the chipping motion. If you think of your arms as hands on a clock, you should take the club back so your left arm points to approximately 9 o'clock. (See illustration.) On the follow-through, your right arm should point to approximately 3 o'clock. When the clubface meets the ball, the clubshaft should be vertical and your hands should be directly over the ball.

In pitching, a constant, light grip pressure throughout the swing is vitally important. Think of letting the club swing by itself, with your hands gripping only firmly enough to hang on for the ride. This light grip pressure will allow the loft of the club to send the ball into the air, landing softly on the green. *Do not try to "help" the ball into the air by swinging up on the follow-through.* This usually will cause you only to "top" the ball, sending it rolling along the ground.

In pitching, you should stand so the ball is directly below your sternum in the middle of your stance. The pitching grip is the same as the grip you will use for all full-swing shots. This grip promotes a freer use of the wrists, which allows you to hit the ball farther. On pitch shots, swing the club back to about 9 o'clock.

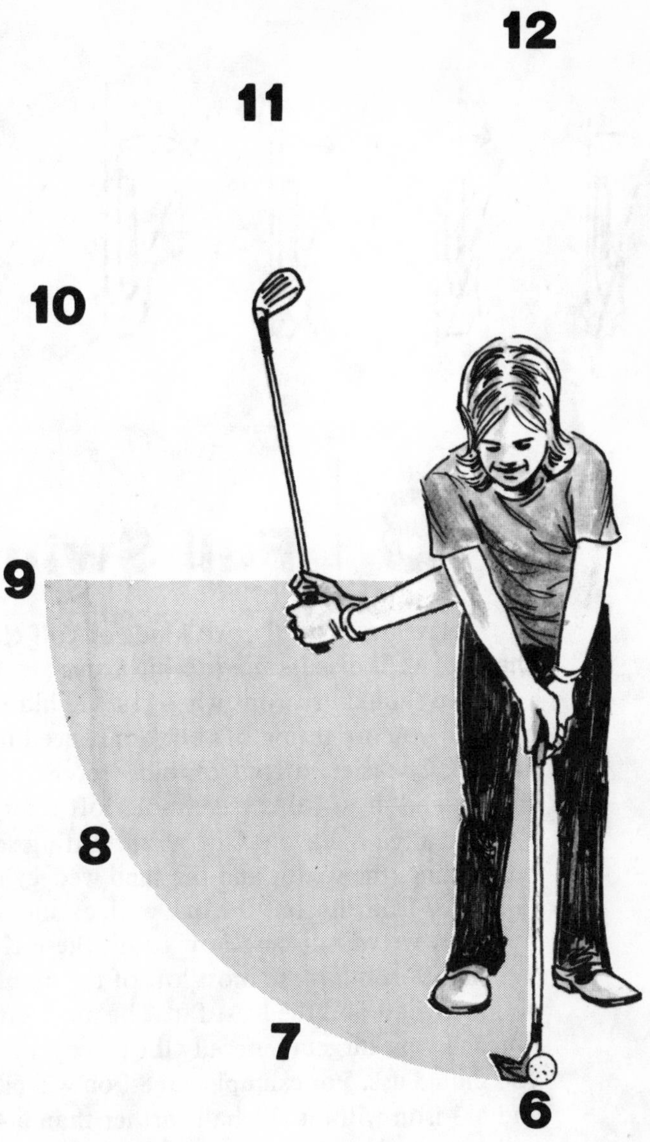

12

11

10

9

8

7

6

Unlike in chipping, in pitching you want a "wristier" (soft-wristed) stroke. Such wristiness will allow the clubhead to swing up more abruptly on the backswing, descend more severely on the downswing, and return up more sharply on the follow-through, which will cause the ball to rise quickly. Also, you can hit the ball farther with a wristy stroke. This is favorable in pitching, since you need to hit the ball farther than you do when chipping.

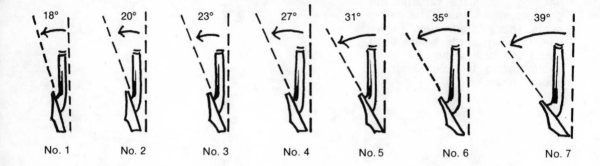

| No. 1 | No. 2 | No. 3 | No. 4 | No. 5 | No. 6 | No. 7 |

8 | Full Swing (Irons)

There are basically two kinds of golf clubs: irons and woods. In this chapter, we'll discuss how to hit irons.

You should use irons when you are hitting approach shots to the green or when you are teeing off but don't need maximum distance. Iron clubs are usually easier to control than woods, because the shafts on irons are shorter and most irons have more loft than most woods.

We already have talked about hitting some iron clubs in the chapter on pitching (the wedge and the sand wedge) and in the chapter on chipping (6-iron, 7-iron, 8-iron, 9-iron, wedge, and sand wedge). In this chapter, however, we will discuss how to hit these clubs their full distances.

The 9-iron has the most loft of the numbered irons. Therefore, it will go the highest and the least far. The more distance you need to hit the ball to reach your target (generally the green), the lower the number of the iron you should use. For example, an 8-iron will hit the ball farther than a 9-iron, and a 3-iron will hit the ball farther than a 4-iron. There are also 2-irons and 1-irons, but until you are a very good player, you need not concern yourself with hitting those clubs.

The correct stance with most irons is similar to the stance for the pitching wedge. The main differences are that the ball should be positioned slightly toward your left foot from the middle of your stance (but some people prefer playing the ball right in the middle of their stance), and you should not use an open stance. Both feet should be toeing that imaginary line toward the target.

32

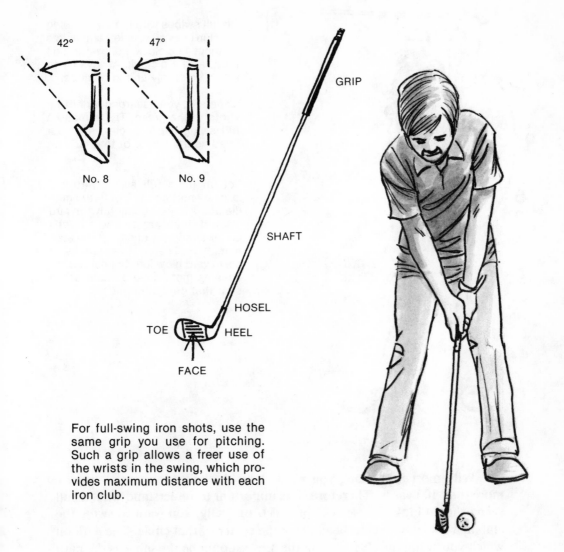

42°   47°

No. 8   No. 9

GRIP

SHAFT

HOSEL

TOE   HEEL

FACE

For full-swing iron shots, use the same grip you use for pitching. Such a grip allows a freer use of the wrists in the swing, which provides maximum distance with each iron club.

The grip for the irons is the same as for pitching. If you are not sure about your grip, ask a golf professional or a good amateur player to check it. It is very important to have a correct grip and to hold the club the same way every time.

For a full swing with the irons, you should take the club back until your left arm points to about 11 o'clock. On the follow-through, your right arm should point at least to 1 o'clock. But a fuller follow-through is fine.

On full swings with the irons, swing the club back so your left arm points to about 11 o'clock. Follow through to at least 1 o'clock. Always try to swing smoothly and in balance.

Generally, you use irons for hitting shots to the green. Try to make a full swing like a circle, with your head as the center of that circle.

Set up for a full swing with the irons by putting the ball in the middle of the stance or slightly forward (toward the target) and directly under or slightly ahead of the sternum. This setup encourages a downward blow into the ball, which ensures more solid contact and a shot that gets airborne.

With most iron shots, you want to hit the ball a long way—usually more than 100 yards. Therefore, it is important to understand what a full swing should look like (see Chapter 11). Basically, you want to swing the club in a circle, with your head being the center of that circle. The path on which you swing the club back in the circle should be the same as the path on which you swing the club forward into the ball. As you begin to hit full-swing iron shots, remember that a good golf swing is a smooth swing. It's okay to swing hard at the ball as long as you keep your swing smooth. For instance, you don't want to make a fast back swing and then a slow forward swing, or vice versa. A good way to know if you are swinging smoothly is to check that you are swinging in balance. If you feel as if you might fall down as you swing or just after you swing, you are not swinging in balance and should try to swing more smoothly.

Another important factor in making a good full swing is a correct weight shift. On the back swing, you should feel as if your weight moves to your right foot. And on the forward swing, it should move to your left foot. Do not let your body do the opposite—called a *reverse weight shift*—where you finish the swing with your weight on your right foot.

With irons, you should make contact with the ball as the club is moving slightly downward on the forward swing. You do not want to catch the ball on the upswing, though this is a common tendency because golfers instinctively try to ''help'' the ball into the air by swinging up at impact.

Because an iron already has loft built into its face, if the club is moving even with or slightly downward to the ground at impact, the ball will automatically go into the air when the club strikes it.

The clubhead, then, should take a thin, shallow divot (a piece of turf from the ground) after hitting the ball. Such a downward type of blow will better ensure solid contact with the ball, especially when it is sitting tight to the ground where there is not much grass.

After making this downward blow through the ball, make a full follow-through, with the clubhead going toward your target. Such a full follow-through will ensure that the club is moving as fast as possible when it meets the ball, which is necessary to achieve maximum distance.

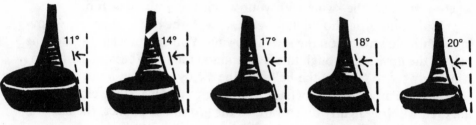

No. 1   No. 2   No. 3   No. 4   No. 5

9 | Full Swing (Woods)

The fairway woods (usually the 3-, 4-, and 5-wood) are used for hitting the ball from the fairway when you need maximum distance or from the tee when you don't need maximum distance.

If you are hitting a fairway wood from the fairway, you need to have a good *lie* (the term for the ball sitting on the turf). Sometimes you can use a fairway wood (especially the 4- and 5-wood) from the rough.

The swing for a fairway wood differs slightly from the full swing for an iron. First, in the setup you should stand a little taller to the ball (stand up straighter rather than bending over) and position it farther left (toward the target), opposite your left heel. This ball position allows you to make more of a sweeping motion with the fairway woods. You want to sweep the ball off the ground without taking a divot (a piece of turf) along with it. Some players take a slight divot with the fairway woods. It is better to do that than to pull up as the club meets the ball, which often causes a low shot that only rolls along the ground.

Because the shaft in a fairway wood is longer than in an iron, the fairway woods sometimes are more difficult to hit. If you find this to be the case, try using only a 5-wood at first and try *choking up on the grip* (put your hands closer to the metal part of the shaft), until you start making solid contact. But don't be afraid to hit the fairway woods. For some peo-

36

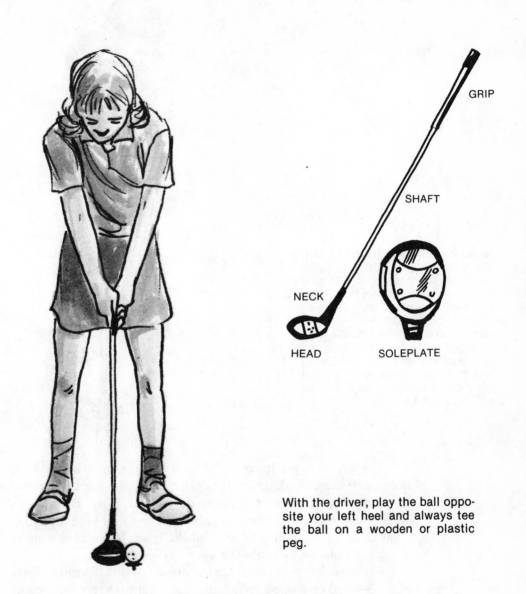

GRIP

SHAFT

NECK

HEAD

SOLEPLATE

With the driver, play the ball opposite your left heel and always tee the ball on a wooden or plastic peg.

ple they are actually easier to play than irons, because you *can* sweep the ball. And you don't have to hit down into the ground, which takes more hand and arm strength.

Lots of modern golfers use 6- and 7-woods (more loft than a 5-wood) and trouble woods, which have metal *runners* along the bottom of the clubhead that allow the club to slide through the grass more easily.

37

When you set up to hit with a fairway wood, position the ball opposite your left heel, closer toward the target than with an iron. Also, because the shaft in a fairway wood is longer than in an iron, you need to stand "taller" to the ball, or more upright. This setup and ball position allow you to swing the clubhead more level to the ground so you can "sweep" the ball off the ground and into the air.

The driver is the longest club and hits the ball the farthest. Because of these two characteristics, it often is the most fun to hit. For most people, however, it is also the hardest. Why? Because the longer shaft makes it harder to control, the shape of the face makes it easier to hit the ball off-line, and the lesser loft makes it more difficult to hit the ball into the air.

Many golfers never even use the driver, opting instead to drive with a 3-wood or 4-wood, which they can hit into the air more easily and hit straighter. You may want to wait until you have played several months—or even a year or so—before trying to hit the driver.

When you do start playing with the driver, you should use it off the tee on holes where you need as much distance as possible (long par 4's and par 5's, for instance). Only use it on par 3's if there is little trouble (bunkers or water) around the green and you truly need maximum distance to reach the green.

Use the driver from the tee on long par 4's and par 5's, where you need maximum distance. If the hole is very narrow (with trees or water on both sides of the fairway, for instance), it might be better to tee off with a 3-wood, 4-wood, or even with an iron, all of which are easier to control than the driver.

With the driver, you should position the ball opposite your left heel and always tee the ball on a wooden or plastic peg (called a *tee*). Tee the ball high enough so that its center is even with the top of the driver's clubhead.

The driver is the only club with which you want to contact the ball slightly on the upswing (with the clubhead moving level to the ground or slightly upward at impact). This motion will give the ball maximum carry and roll, which translates into maximum distance.

10 | Specialty Shots

Invariably when you play golf, you hit the ball into *sand bunkers* (also called *sand traps*). Even the best players in the world hit the ball into trouble sometimes. Some players are intimidated by sand bunkers, but they needn't be. Escaping from sand is actually very easy.

Good sand play is a result of two things: (1) having the correct type of club (a sand wedge), and (2) using the correct technique. First, let's look at the sand wedge.

Ideally, you want a club whose sole is shaped like the one in the illustration. The sole on a sand wedge is called the *flange*. You need a sand wedge whose flange is shaped in such a manner that the leading edge is higher than the trailing edge when the clubshaft is vertical to the ground. This is called *bounce* on a sand wedge and is what allows the club to slide or bounce through the sand easily.

Generally, the more bounce on your sand wedge (the higher the leading edge compared with the trailing edge), the easier the club will slide through the sand. You don't want a sand wedge with too much bounce, however, because it then becomes difficult to use from the fairway for pitching. Find a good sand wedge (one that has sufficient bounce and is the right length for you) and have a local golf professional check it to be sure it suits your game and build.

The main principle to remember when hitting from a sand bunker near the green is that *the clubhead never touches the ball*. Actually, the clubhead should slide *under* the ball, sending the ball out of the bunker on a cushion of sand. This technique is better than trying to "chip" the ball out cleanly (as some unknowing players try to do) because it provides a greater margin for error. You can take a lot of sand or just a little. As long as you make a full swing and a full follow-through, the ball usually will float out of the bunker nicely.

So here's what to do when your ball is in a sand bunker:

The clubhead of the sand wedge should slide under the ball, sending it out on a cushion of sand. The clubhead should never actually touch the ball on a normal sand shot from near the green.

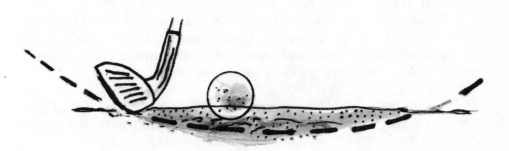

1. Set up as you would for a pitch shot (slightly open stance with your left foot pulled back from the imaginary line across your toes toward the target).

2. Dig your feet into the sand about half an inch or so. This keeps you from slipping and puts you slightly below the level of the sand so it's easier for the clubhead to slide under the ball.

3. Open the clubface in relation to the line across your toes so it is aimed more toward the target. Open the clubface by turning it to the right first and then taking your normal grip. Don't simply turn your hands to the right.

4. Make a slow and full swing, allowing the clubhead to enter the sand two to four inches behind the ball, and follow through fully so the ball flies gently out of the bunker.

Remember that a sand bunker is a hazard (see Chapter 4), which means that you cannot let the club touch the sand until you start your downswing. Because of this, you might want to take your grip (with the clubface open) and make your practice swing outside the bunker.

Out of the Rough

When your ball happens to go into the taller grass near the fairway (called the *rough*), it is sometimes difficult to hit it. In taller grass the ball tends to sit down, making it harder to contact with the clubface. There are some adjustments you can make in your setup, swing, and club selection that can help you hit the ball more cleanly.

First, check the lie. If the ball is sitting low in the grass, you will need to use a more lofted club (a 7-iron instead of a 5-iron, for example). The extra loft helps to get the ball airborne.

Second, you need to set up to the ball in such a way that it will be easier to strike the ball solidly. To do this, position the ball farther back in your stance (more opposite your right foot). This ball position will encourage you to make a more upright swing, which will help you to make cleaner contact.

Finally, you should aim more to the right when hitting out of the rough. The taller grass causes the clubface to *close* (point to the left of the target) through impact, promoting a pull or a hook.

Because blades of grass tend to get between the clubface and the ball, the ball often flies with little spin (like a knuckleball in baseball), which will make it roll farther when it hits the ground. So you must allow for this.

Sometimes a 4-wood, 5-wood, or trouble wood is easier to hit out of the rough than an iron. The sole of a wood is smoother and glides through the grass, whereas an iron can get tangled up. But you should use a wood from the rough only (1) when the grass is not too tall, and (2) when the distance to your target requires the length of a wood shot.

If you're in the rough near the green, a sand wedge often is easier to hit than a pitching wedge. As in the sand, the flange on the sand wedge glides through the rough, while the sharper edge of the pitching wedge sometimes digs in too deeply. Also, because the sand wedge has more loft than the pitching wedge, the ball will come out higher and land more softly on the green.

When you're in the rough, set up so the ball is positioned farther back in your stance. Use a more lofted club than you normally would and make a more upright back swing. Then strike down sharply on the back of the ball or just behind the ball. The shot will have little spin, causing it to roll farther than normal.

11 | Final Swing Thoughts

The golf swing can be a complicated motion if you let it become complicated. The best golfers, however, try to keep their swings as simple as possible—no unnecessary movements. Generally, the fewer swing thoughts you are concerned with, the better. And if you are working on a particular swing thought, think about it only on the practice range. When you are on the golf course, try to let your swing happen automatically. Think only about your target, alignment, and the tempo of your swing when you are playing.

Most good players have what is called an *inside-out swing path*. In reality, they swing inside the target line on the back swing to down the line at impact to back inside on the follow-through. To understand this concept more clearly, think of a giant clockface flat on the ground with your ball in the center of that face. Pretend your target is 12 o'clock and you are standing on the 9 o'clock side of the center, facing 3 o'clock.

On your back swing, you should swing the club toward 7 o'clock. On your forward swing, you should swing the club toward 1 o'clock. This is what is meant by swinging "inside out," and if the clubface is facing the target (12 o'clock) at impact, your shot will start toward 1 o'clock, hooking (curving left) back toward your target (12 o'clock).

The best shot shape for young golfers is one that starts slightly to the right of the target and hooks back to the target. This is the ideal shot because the ball will travel farther—it will *fly* farther and will *roll* farther. Until you're older and stronger, a controlled hook is the optimum shot to develop.

A shot that hooks is caused when the clubface is aligned left of the swing path at impact. If you are having trouble with a slice, don't worry. Simply swing along the 7 o'clock to 1 o'clock path. As the clubhead nears the ball, feel as if your right hand is turning over your left hand. A simple drill to perfect this motion (called *release*) is the toe-up-to-toe-up drill. Here's how it works:

44

With the ball teed, take a 5- or 7-iron and address the ball normally. Then, using only your hands and wrists, swing the club back so the shaft is perpendicular to the ground and the toe of the clubhead is pointing toward the sky. Again, using only your hands and wrists, swing the club down and through, hitting the ball off the tee. Follow through only far enough so that the shaft is again perpendicular to the ground and the toe is again pointing toward the sky. This drill forces you to turn your right hand over your left at impact, which is the feeling you need in order to hook the ball. Practice this drill periodically on the range until your full shots start curving from right to left.

One final swing thought: Never underestimate the importance of a good grip. If you are not sure about your grip, ask a local pro to check it to be certain it's correct. Or look in golf magazines and books for pictures of the best players and copy their grips. If you start with a good grip now, golf will be much easier for you to learn. A good grip is the keystone to a good swing.

12 | Let's Sum Up

Remember that golf is supposed to be fun. After all, it's only a game. Golf is different from other sports in that you call penalties on yourself, you congratulate your opponent when he or she hits a good shot, and console your opponent when he or she hits a bad one. The game is based on the honor system, and it relies on the individual's integrity to make it work.

Etiquette plays a major part in golf. Always be careful not to distract the other players by talking or moving when they are preparing to hit. And always play quickly so you don't hold up the other players in your group or the group behind you. If you are looking for a lost ball or are otherwise playing slowly, ask the group behind to play through. After all, you would want them to do the same for you if they were holding you up.

Above all, golf is a game of sportsmanship.

TOM WATSON (CENTER) IS CONGRATULATED BY
JACK NICKLAUS FOR WINNING THE '77 BRITISH OPEN.

INDEX